100

AMERICAN

FLAGS

100 AMERICAN FLAGS

A UNIQUE COLLECTION OF OLD GLORY MEMORABILIA

COLLECTION & DESIGN BY KIT HINRICHS

TEXT BY DELPHINE HIRASUNA

PHOTOGRAPHY BY TERRY HEFFERNAN

TEN SPEED PRESS

Berkeley

The Continental Congress resolved in 1777 that "the flag of the United States be thirteen stripes, alternate red and white; that the Union be thirteen stars, white in a blue field representing a new constellation." The Revolutionary War–time haste with which this resolution was written left these graphic elements open to broad interpretation. ★ Far from being a static symbol, the American flag has been rendered with stars in countless configurations, especially as a new star was added each time a state joined the Union. Not only did the "constellation" vary from circles to rows, gaps were left on the blue canton by practical flag makers anticipating additional stars as more territories earned statehood. ★ It was not until Congress passed official standards in 1912 that the flag took on a fixed appearance. Still, more than a century without guidelines established a tradition of personalizing the Stars and Stripes, letting it speak not just for a nation, but for an ideal, a value, a way of life. ★ Over the years, the American flag has been raised high in wartime triumph and peacetime celebration; burned in fervent protest; shown proudly on quilts, pillowcases, and bags; appropriated by commercial interests to sell goods; and honored every Fourth of July to celebrate America's independence. ★ This range of expressions has fascinated graphic designer Kit Hinrichs, who has amassed a collection of more than five thousand Stars and Stripes objects, from Civil War banners to Native American moccasins. ★ *100 American Flags* provides a glimpse of this spectacular collection and the stories behind each object.

STARS &

THE EVOLVING

ICON FROM

IN 1777 UN

STRIPES

G AMERICAN

TS CREATION

TIL TODAY

Centennial Flag

In 1876, a flag maker created this flag to mark the one hundredth anniversary of the signing of the Declaration of Independence and founding of the United States. Although widely known, the banner is not considered an official American flag since it features eighty-one stars instead of thirty-eight, the number of states in the Union at the time.

Regimental Flag

Upon being disbanded, the 71st New York Volunteer Infantry (also known as Sickles' Brigade) created this thirty-five-star flag to commemorate the major battles of the Civil War in which the regiment participated.

Assorted Patriotic Pins

Around 1891, two inventions—a machine that could cut faceted glass and an automated metal plating device—made the use of rhinestones affordable for all types of costume jewelry. The perfect accessory for patriotic occasions, rhinestone flag pins of red, white, and blue became the rage by the early twentieth century and have remained popular ever since.

FLAG NO. 4

Crocheted Flag

During World War I
and II, even crochet
patterns printed in
women's magazines
featured the American
flag and wartime
slogans.

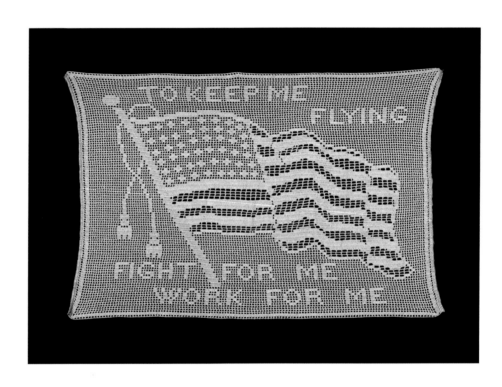

FLAG NO. 5

**Patriotic
Pillow Cover**

Crocheting was all the
rage in the early part of
the twentieth century,
reaching its peak around
the time of the First
World War. Patriotic
themes were particularly
popular then, since
more than four million
Americans—over
25 percent of the entire
U.S. male population
between the ages of
eighteen and thirty-
one—served in the
United States Army
during the Great War.

13

**Stamp
Cancellation Mark**

The stamp cancellation mark used by the United States Postal Service in the late 1800s depicted a full waving flag. By the late 1920s, the postal service abbreviated the mark to just waving stripes, still used today.

Postage Flag

During World War II, an unknown artist assembled this flag from postage stamps and cancellation marks on envelopes. The stars in the canton bear the cancellation mark from the capital of each of the forty-eight states that were in the Union at the time.

Flag Holder

Shaped much like the newel post of a staircase, this flag holder was used by stores in the late nineteenth century to display handheld flags for sale.

**Lady Liberty
Flag Holder**

The head of the Statue of Liberty, presented to the United States by France in 1886, quickly became a symbol for American values and an apt way for shopkeepers to display the flag.

**The Non-Melting
Pot Flag**

For the bicentennial,
Italian-born designer
Massimo Vignelli, who
lives in Manhattan,
created this flag out
of ethnic newspapers
published in New
York City. Vignelli
portrays America not
as a melting pot, but
instead as a place that
tolerates and supports
the coexistence of
different cultures and
opinions.

Tied-Silk Flag

In the 1930s, an
unknown artist created
a knotted-grid mat
from gold silk thread,
then tied and clipped
red, white, and blue
silk threads in a pattern
that formed an image
of the flag.

and Army of the Republic, celebrating the Union veterans of the Civil War, held in Salt Lake City, Utah, in August 1909. At the time, the G.A.R. had 220,600 members.

Fourth of July "Cap" Stick

Uncle Sam Party Hat

Accordian Party Hat

Washington's Birthday Party Favor

Party Favor

Clicker

Noisemaker

Patriotic Party Paraphernalia

Noisemakers, party favors, and other objects with Stars and Stripes themes have been a part of every Fourth of July celebration since the country declared its independence from England in 1776.

Party Horn

Statue of Liberty Party Horn

Fourth of July Party Horn

Striped Party Horn

Parade Parasol

BUGLE HORN

Scout Knife

The Stars and Stripes figure prominently in Boy Scout gear, along with the teaching of loyalty, patriotism, and duty to country. Part of Scout training is the Pledge of Allegiance and the proper handling and respect for the flag.

Fund-Raising Product

Circa 1930, flag manufacturers would help Boy Scout troops earn money to buy a flag by providing them with a free box of thirty paper flag pins. The scouts would in turn sell the lapel pins for ten cents a piece, raising three dollars per box—enough to buy a 3- by 5-foot cotton flag.

Needle Case

The top of this needle
kit is made with a petit
point stitch sewn onto
a felt back with a
beaded star.

FLAG NO. 28

Penny-Stitch Flag

About the time of
the Civil War, thrifty
homemakers began
using wool scrap
threads, sewn onto
a wool background,
to make decorative
coverings and wall
hangings. Pennies
were used as a circular
template, hence the
name *penny stitch*.

FLAG NO. 29

Friendship Kimono

This kimono, with flags of both the United States and Japan, was probably created in 1912, the year that Mayor Ozaki of Tokyo presented President Taft with three thousand cherry blossom trees to be planted along the Potomac as a gesture of friendship.

Patriotic Flag Dress

With four million
Americans drafted into
the Army during World
War I, patriotic fervor
ran high. A mother
made this dress for her
little girl to wear in a
Fourth of July parade,
circa 1917.

Cornhusk Bag

Designed for the tourist trade, this cornhusk bag was made by Pueblo Indians. Over the centuries, the Pueblos mastered the technique of wrapping the inner layer of cornhusks tightly around twine in a false embroidery technique. The husks would be dyed before being woven into bags, hats, and belts.

Navajo Chevrolet Flag Weaving

After the railroad reached Gallup, New Mexico, in 1882, Navajo weavers were encouraged to create rugs and patterns that appealed to non-Indian buyers. This rug once hung in a Chevrolet dealership in Gallup.

FLAG NO. 33

Woodland Indian Whimsy

Forced into reservations, Native Americans struggled to survive by creating craftwork for the non-Indian tourist trade. Around the early twentieth century, Woodland Indians made small beaded "whimsies" and sold them as souvenirs to tourists at Niagara Falls.

Beaded Flag Violin Case

This elaborately beaded violin case bears the initials R and B, which stand for the name of its owner, Rubin Bass. The symbolism and style of beading are representative of the work done by Brule Sioux in South Dakota. "Rubin Bass, Elk Falls, Feb. 11, 1891" is inscribed in deer hide on the back of the violin case.

**Lakota
Gauntlet Gloves**

Gauntlet gloves intended for commercial sales to non–Native Americans often featured realistic images rather than geometric designs. This pair of gloves was made by Lakota Indians during the reservation period that began in the late nineteenth century. The flag and domestic flower design was probably inspired by an image seen in a magazine.

**Cheyenne Flag
Moccasins**

Moccasins and other items such as armbands, breastplates, and pouches were often elaborately beaded by Cheyenne Indians. These moccasins feature lane or lazy stitch beadwork, a method by which eight or so beads are strung together then sewn tightly onto the animal hide surface.

36

Navajo Weaving

This Navajo flag
weaving, representing
a forty-nine-star grid,
was created in 1959 to
commemorate Alaska's
entry into the Union.
Forty-nine-star flags
are relatively rare
because of Hawaii's
statehood the following
year, raising the
number of stars to fifty.

**Second U.S.
Calvary Guidon**

Military units would
fall into formation
behind a guidon, or
flag held aloft on a
staff. This guidon was
made for the Second
U.S. Calvary, which
fought in the Battle of
Gettysburg in the Civil
War as well as in Cuba
during the Spanish-
American War. Printed
in 1890, this forty-two-
star flag immediately
became invalid due
to the last-minute
admission of Idaho as
the forty-third state on
July 3, 1890.

Tobacciana

Between 1890 and
1910, the American
Tobacco Trust waged
a major marketing
campaign to
monopolize all forms
of tobacco production.
The effort gave the
American Tobacco
Company control of
roughly 90 percent of
the tobacco production
in the United States
and Europe by 1903.
To woo smokers, the
company offered all
kinds of premiums,
including cigar "felts,"
cigarette cards, cigar
bands, and decorated
boxes. A favorite theme
was the Stars and
Stripes, which appealed
to the consumers'
sense of patriotism and
reminded them that
tobacco originated in
America, where the
best tobacco products
were still being
produced.

**Presidential
Cigar Bands**

Thousands of cigar
and cigarette brands
existed in the early
twentieth century.
Tobacco companies
vied for repeat
customers by offering
promotional items
that they would want
to collect, such as this
series of presidential
cigar bands.

Victorian Trade Card

In the late nineteenth century, companies distributed decorative trade cards to promote their products. Sewing machine makers often issued cards featuring sweet little girls to imply that the machines made the task so easy that even a child could sew. Women and girls collected these cards to paste in their scrapbooks.

Fruit Can Label

Before Congress enacted an official code of flag etiquette in 1923, advertisers wrapped their brand image around the flag and all the patriotic values that the public connects to it.

Patriotic Airplane Livery

Although the Sopwith Camel—the plane flown by
Snoopy in the *Peanuts* comic strips—may be the
best remembered military aircraft of the first World
War, the French-built SPAD XIII was flown by
many more American pilots. Most famous was the
"Ace of Aces," Eddie Rickenbacker, who flew
with the 94th Aero Squadron. This squadron's
insignia was a hat in a ring, because they were
the first American squadron to "toss their hat into
the ring" and begin operations in World War I.

Flag Domino Tiles

The thirty-eight stars
shown on the flag
on the back side of
these domino tiles
offer a clue that the
set was probably
created sometime
between 1877 and
1890, the year that five
more states entered
the Union.

FLAG NO. 45

Stix Puzzle

Flag Stix puzzles helped
young children increase
their dexterity, identify
familiar icons, and use
logic to assemble the
sticks to recreate the
flag. Stix puzzles were
available in the flags
of many nations.

FLAG NO. 46

Flag Bearer Toy Soldiers

A flag bearer is an integral figure in every set of toy soldiers. Over the centuries, toy soldiers have been cast from metal, carved out of wood, and made from composition (sawdust and glue), and then hand-painted. Among collectors, the flag bearer is highly coveted for the symbolism of his role and the intricate workmanship required to reproduce the flag.

Mickey Mouse

The American flag and Walt Disney's Mickey Mouse are two of the most recognizable symbols of the United States. The debut of the first Mickey Mouse film in 1928 made the animated character an instant star, with fans seeing the best of America in Mickey's optimism and resourcefulness.

Bed Doll

Bed dolls were not meant to be children's playthings; rather, they were used as decorative accents. As a result, they were rather large and delicate and were often made of exceptionally fine materials.

Uncle Sam
Folding Fan

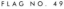

Over the years, flag fans have been made in a number of cylindrical forms, including the likeness of Uncle Sam. The body of this Uncle Sam is made of papier-mâché and the head is of clay.

52

Cigar Cockade Fans

The patriotic cigar
cockade fan was
introduced at the 1893
Columbian Exhibition
in Chicago. This fan
style is called "cockade"
because when the top of
the faux cigar is pulled
up, a full 360-degree
fan reveals itself.

Uncle Sam Bank

David and Susan Kirk
created this mechanical
Uncle Sam bank in
the late 1970s. Uncle
Sam's eyes recede and
his tongue extends to
receive the coins. David
Kirk is the creator of the
much-loved Miss Spider
children's book series.

FLAG NO. 52

Homemade Puzzle

Crafted from scrap
materials, this
homemade puzzle is
designed to teach a
young child how to
match sizes, shapes,
and colors.

Pencil Assemblage

For an American
Institute of Graphic Arts
exhibition and auction,
Texas-based graphic
designer Chris Hill
created this original
piece out of twenty-four
hundred red, white, and
blue pencils.

Pencil Box

Uncle Sam and the
Stars and Stripes
decorate this pencil
container designed for
schoolchildren.

Tattooed Sailor

Sailor William Ray, who served in the United
States Navy circa September 1917, according to
the date tattooed on his back, embellished his
torso and arms with patriotic images and nautical
themes. His tattoo art was photographed and
printed as postcards.

**Junior
Mechanics Flag**

The Junior Order
of United American
Mechanics, an anti-
immigrant fraternal
organization formed
in Germantown,
Pennsylvania, in 1853,
centered its symbol—
a compass and mason's
square framing labor's
arm and hammer—
amid the flag's canton
of stars.

60

**Twenty-Nine-
Star Flag**

This twenty-nine-star
parade flag from
1847 presents the
stars in a medallion
configuration with the
center star larger than
the others. Printed on
buckram, the flag was
probably produced
for use in James K.
Polk's campaign for
president.

Army Blanket

On the eve of the
United States's entry
into the First World
War, a soldier whose
initials were E. H.
embroidered patriotic
images on an army
blanket for his parents.

**Pearl Harbor
Blanket**

A mother's grief
for a son killed on
the USS *Arizona* in
1941 is expressed
on this crocheted
blanket, which shows
battleships, warplanes,
machine guns, and
pistols, along with
the exact time of
the attack on
Pearl Harbor.

FLAG NO. 61

Hickam Field Flag

This flag flew over Hickam Field, adjacent to the Pearl Harbor U.S. naval base in Hawaii. The slogan on the flag was the rallying cry in the war against Japan and also was used to encourage citizens to buy war bonds.

Admiral Dewey Pin

This pin and silk flag
featuring a brass bust
of Admiral George
Dewey commemorated
the Navy's Great White
Fleet. As president of
the General Board
of the Navy, Dewey
was instrumental in
developing a greater
naval presence for the
United States, including
a global voyage of the
Great White Fleet in
1907 to demonstrate
America's sea power.

FLAG NO. 63

**Eagle, Flag,
and Shield Label**

After defeating the
Spanish fleet in the
Battle of Manila during
the Spanish-American
War of 1898, Admiral
George Dewey was
viewed as a national
hero, with his picture
even appearing on
a whiskey flask. His
popularity prompted
him to run for president
in 1900, but he quickly
withdrew his candidacy.

FLAG NO. 64

Woven Ribbons

Starting in 1862, political
ribbons began featuring
finely detailed words and
images thanks to a silk-
weaving technique called
Stevengraph, invented
by the English ribbon
maker Thomas Stevens
using a Jacquard loom.
The first Stevengraphs
appeared as bookmarks,
and were later followed
by other formats such as
postcards. This selection
includes Stevengraphs
as well as traditional
printed, stamped, and
embroidered ribbons.

Handlebar Ornament

Airplanes were recent inventions when this pre–World War I bicycle ornament was created. It was designed to fly merrily from its mount on the handlebar, while the propeller spun.

Soldiers' Portraits

Soldiers shipping off for the First World War would sit for portraits that were printed with a decorative frame as a single celluloid unit. The unbreakable frames made it easy to send the portraits back to families at home.

COREA
1871
BYL
BATTERY

ND, OR BY SEA!

RODGERS.

FLAG NO. 67

Rodgers's Battle Flag

This flag flew on ships commanded by Admiral John Rodgers during the Civil War and the Korean Conflict of 1871. The banner first saw action in 1861 when then-Captain Rodgers's ship came under cannon fire from Confederate troops. For his bravery, Rodgers was promoted to rear admiral and presented with the flag. In 1871, he was put in charge of the Asiatic Fleet, which fought several battles in Korea. After the signing of the Korean treaty, Rodgers presented the flag to a lieutenant who had risked his life rescuing it during the storming of a fort on the Seoul River.

Poker Chips

National pride ran
high during America's
centennial celebrations
in 1876. Manufacturers
embellished all manner
of products with
the American flag,
including these clay
poker chips.

**Victory
Playing Cards**

Although playing cards
was a diversion from
the war, the cause
was never far from
anyone's mind. During
World War II, card
decks usually pictured
patriotic themes. Here,
Hitler and Mussolini
are the Jokers.

Commemorative Spoons

Sold at world's fairs, in tourist gift shops, and at special events, commemorative spoons have been popular collectibles for more than a century. Patriotic motifs have been perennial best-sellers.

Eagle and Shield, Cloisonné

Crossed Flags, Silver and Enamel

Sesquicentennial, Sterling Silver and Enamel

Battleship Maine, Silver and Enamel

Oklahoma, Silver and Enamel

Battleship Maine, Silver and Enamel

Eagle and Shield, Etched Silver and Cloisonné

Army and Navy, Gold Plate and Enamel

Panama Canal, Silver and Cloisonné

Forty-Eight-Star Flag, Sterling Silver and Enamel

Uncle Sam, Silver and Cloisonné

Chicago, Silver and Enamel

Ladies' Compacts

The designs for ladies'
compacts ranged from
austere brass and wood
from World War I
and World War II to
glamorous rhinestone
and elegant enamel,
put out for the nation's
bicentennial.

FLAG NO. 72

Shotgun Shell Case

A one-of-a-kind
piece, this shotgun
shell case was
lovingly inlaid with
hunting dogs and
a forty-eight-star
flag by an amateur
woodworker in
the 1940s.

Weather Vanes

Weather vanes were once a common sight on barns across rural America. The nation's flag was a popular icon because its broad, flat surface easily caught the wind. These printed-tin vanes date from World War I and World War II. The holes in some of the stars were made by farm boys using the fixtures for target practice.

"Solid as the Oak"
Pillow Cover

This embroidered pillow case from around 1910 was probably made from a pattern that appeared in a women's magazine or was printed on cloth to be individually stitched at home.

Outsider Art Flag

This primitive drawing
on tin is one of many
pieces made by
R. A. Miller, a Georgia
farmer and cotton
mill worker. Although
stricken by glaucoma,
he continues as one
of the better known
outsider artists,
painting tin cutouts
and whirligigs often
with patriotic themes.

Crazy Quilt

Crazy quilts became
the rage after the
Philadelphia Centennial
Exposition of 1876.
A way for women to
show off their stitching
skills, these quilts were
typically assembled from
silk, velvet, and broad
fabrics cut in random
shapes. Their design
often incorporated bits
of cultural lore, patriotic
symbols, and family
history.

McKinley Quilt

This quilt, constructed
of uncut flags and flag
bunting, was made
in memory of William
McKinley, who became
president of the United
States in 1897 and
was assassinated by
an anarchist named
Leon Czolgosz in 1901.
The initials W. R. H.
are those of the
quilt maker.

Centennial Quilt

Created to mark the
nation's centennial, this
quilt features thirty-six-
star flags, even though
thirty-eight states were
officially part of the
Union at the time.

FLAG NO. 79

Toy Biplane

This tin toy biplane was made in Japan prior to World War II for sale in the U.S. market.

FLAG NO. 80

**Lucky Lindy
Folk Art Flag**

This one-of-a-kind chenille piece by José Santos of New Rochelle, New York, commemorates the first nonstop east and west crossing of the Atlantic by American and French flyers. Rife with information, the wall hanging incorporates photographs of Charles Lindbergh and the two French pilots and their national flags, with names and flight records embroidered along the border.

FLAG NO. 82

**Red Star Line
Folding Fan**

This is a promotional fan from the Red Star Line shipping company, which between 1873 and 1935 transported almost three million passengers from Antwerp, Belgium, to North America. Many immigrants who passed through New York's Ellis Island came here on a Red Star vessel.

ANTWERP·NEW·YORK

Lands' End Quilt

Commissioned by
Lands' End to create
a flag quilt design for
the cover of its catalog,
graphic designer
and flag collector
Kit Hinrichs made an
assemblage from his
favorite nineteenth
century flag designs.
Quilting artist Sonya
Lee Barrington then
hand-dyed the fabric,
assembled the pieces,
and quilted Hinrichs's
design into a wall
hanging.

**Nevada
Statehood Quilt**

A ten-woman quilting
circle commemorated
Nevada's entry as the
thirty-sixth state in the
Union by sewing this
satin thirty-six-star flag
quilt in a log cabin
pattern. The quilt later
hung in the offices of
the chief of police in
San Francisco.

94

Flag Money Clip

Although official flag
etiquette bans the
use of the American
flag for advertising
purposes, it does not
forbid displaying it on
all kinds of products,
including money clips.

FLAG NO. 85

Dollar Flag

Artist Ray Beldner
is known for turning
money into art, in
this case sewing
157 one-dollar bills
together, alternating
front and back sides,
to create this American
flag. His series titled
"Counterfeit" remakes
masterpieces by
Duchamp, Warhol,
and others from U.S.
currency.

FLAG NO. 87

**Greek and
American Flags**

A Greek immigrant
made this folksy art
piece from beads wired
to a painted vegetable
crate to celebrate the
friendship between
Greece and the United
States. The plaque
bears the Greek
inscription "liberty."

FLAG NOS. 88 & 89

**World War I
Postcards**

These postcards were
produced in Belgium
during the First World
War. They feature the
flags of Allied nations
and the U.S. flag.

Peace Flag

Over the years,
different groups have
substituted the Stars
and Stripes on the flag
with other symbols,
including the peace
sign, to support
their causes.

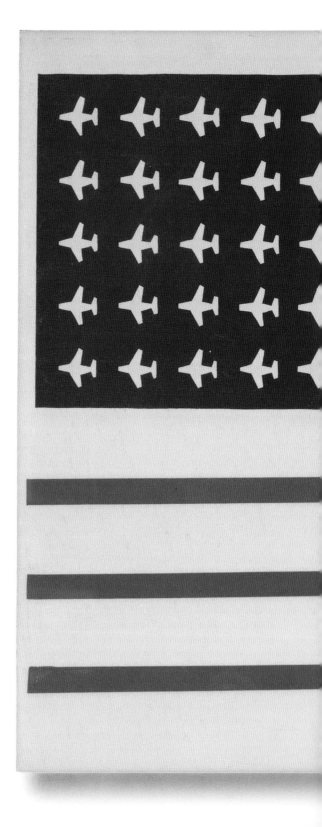

Anti-War Placard

During the Vietnam
War, this placard,
featuring silhouettes of
rifles and warplanes,
was produced on
the campus of the
University of California
at Berkeley.

Union Shield

This wooden emblem
is believed to be the
shield for a presidential
campaign train at
the beginning of the
twentieth century.

**Iroquois
Plateau Pouch**

During the early
reservation period
between 1880 and
1920, beadwork arts
flourished among
Plateau people and
were bought by
tourists, collectors,
and museums.

PATENTED AUG 7TH 1888

**Red Flag
Handkerchief**

Although this flag
handkerchief has
thirty-six stars,
corresponding to 1865,
it was actually created
in 1888 and may
have coincided with
Benjamin Harrison's
run for the presidency.

FLAG NO. 95

**Franco-Anglo-
American Alliance
"Humanity Flag"**

To represent the
Allied powers—Great
Britain, France, and
the United States—of
the First World War,
Albert Hewitt of Mount
Vernon, New York,
designed and patented
a variation of the
Stars and Stripes,
turning the usual blue
canton into the French
Tricolor and substituting
rows of the British
Union Jack for the red
stripes. He named his
amalgamation the
"humanity flag."

FLAG NO. 96

Patriotic Buttons

The late 1890s saw the introduction of inexpensive patriotic buttons made by placing a thin piece of celluloid protective covering over printed paper and then wrapping it around a metal disk.

PROTECTION VS. FREE TRADE.

FOR PRESIDENT.
BENJAMIN HARRISON.
FOR VICE PRESIDENT.
LEVI P. MORTON.

PENSIONS FOR SOLDIERS.

AID FOR FREE SCHOOLS.

Patented June 28 1888.

A.S. Rosenthal & Co. N.Y.

Benjamin Harrison Handkerchief

With thirty-eight states in the Union when Benjamin Harrison ran for president in 1888, campaigning had become a cross-continental effort. This made political giveaways such as this printed handkerchief an essential for promoting the party platform.

Political Handkerchiefs

Engraved copper cylinders enabled whole lengths of bleached cotton cloth and silk to be printed quickly and inexpensively. Campaign handkerchiefs were then mass produced and blanketed late nineteenth century America.

Uncle Sam Postcard

Popular during the
early twentieth century,
a uniquely Chinese
art form of watercolor
and collage was used
to create this image
of Uncle Sam. Uncle
Sam's attire is made
entirely out of canceled
U.S. stamps.

Living Flag

During and shortly after
the First World War,
a young photographer
named Arthur S. Mole
and his partner,
John D. Thomas, visited
military camps around
the country and created
dozens of "living
photographs." In 1917,
ten thousand cadets
(all saluting) at the
United States Naval
Training Station in
Great Lakes, Illinois,
were assembled on
the parade ground for
this photograph. Mole
stood on an eighty-foot
tower that his assistants
constructed to gain the
proper perspective for
his picture.

A Chronological History

The American flag has changed frequently and dramatically since the Continental Congress resolved on June 14, 1777 "that the flag of the United States be thirteen stripes, alternate red and white; that the Union be thirteen stars, white in a blue field representing a new constellation." The vague wording left much room for graphic interpretation, encouraged further by two Congressional acts. In 1795, Congress decreed that a single star and single stripe be added whenever a new state joined the Union. In 1818, Congress changed its mind, reverting back to thirteen horizontal stripes, alternating red and white, to symbolize the original colonies, with each state represented by a single star. The new star would be added on the Fourth of July following a state's admission to the Union. In 1912, Congress finally legislated official graphic standards for how the flag must appear. Presented here is a chronology of state admissions and one example of how the flag was graphically interpreted at that time.

June 14, 1777 (13 stars)
Delaware
Pennsylvania
New Jersey
Georgia
Connecticut
Massachusetts
Maryland
South Carolina
New Hampshire
Virginia
New York
North Carolina
Rhode Island
★
President Serving under the Flag
George Washington

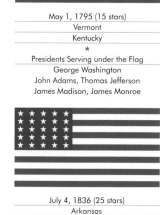

May 1, 1795 (15 stars)
Vermont
Kentucky
★
Presidents Serving under the Flag
George Washington
John Adams, Thomas Jefferson
James Madison, James Monroe

July 4, 1836 (25 stars)
Arkansas
★
Presidents Serving under the Flag
Andrew Jackson
Martin Van Buren

July 4, 1848 (30 stars)
Wisconsin
★
Presidents Serving under the Flag
James K. Polk
Zachary Taylor
Millard Fillmore

July 4, 1851 (31 stars)
California
★
Presidents Serving under the Flag
Millard Fillmore
Franklin Pierce
James Buchanan

July 4, 1858 (32 stars)
Minnesota
★
President Serving under the Flag
James Buchanan

July 4, 1859 (33 stars)
Oregon
★
Presidents Serving under the Flag
James Buchanan
Abraham Lincoln

July 4, 1877 (38 stars)
Colorado
★
Presidents Serving under the Flag
Rutherford B. Hayes, James Garfield
Chester Alan Arthur, Grover Cleveland
Benjamin Harrison

July 4, 1890 (43 stars)
North Dakota
South Dakota
Montana
Washington
Idaho
★
President Serving under the Flag
Benjamin Harrison

July 4, 1891 (44 stars)
Wyoming
★
Presidents Serving under the Flag
Benjamin Harrison
Grover Cleveland

July 4, 1896 (45 stars)
Utah
★
Presidents Serving under the Flag
Grover Cleveland
William McKinley
Theodore Roosevelt

April 13, 1818 (20 stars)

Tennessee, Ohio
Louisiana, Indiana
Mississippi

★

President Serving under the Flag
James Monroe

July 4, 1819 (21 stars)

Illinois

★

President Serving under the Flag
James Monroe

July 4, 1820 (23 stars)

Alabama
Maine

★

President Serving under the Flag
James Monroe

July 4, 1822 (24 stars)

Missouri

★

Presidents Serving under the Flag
James Monroe
John Quincy Adams
Andrew Jackson

July 4, 1837 (26 stars)

Michigan

★

Presidents Serving under the Flag
Martin Van Buren
William Henry Harrison
John Tyler
James K. Polk

July 4, 1845 (27 stars)

Florida

★

President Serving under the Flag
James K. Polk

July 4, 1846 (28 stars)

Texas

★

President Serving under the Flag
James K. Polk

July 4, 1847 (29 stars)

Iowa

★

President Serving under the Flag
James K. Polk

July 4, 1861 (34 stars)

Kansas

★

President Serving under the Flag
Abraham Lincoln

July 4, 1863 (35 stars)

West Virginia

★

Presidents Serving under the Flag
Abraham Lincoln
Andrew Johnson

July 4, 1865 (36 stars)

Nevada

★

President Serving under the Flag
Andrew Johnson

July 4, 1867 (37 stars)

Nebraska

★

Presidents Serving under the Flag
Andrew Johnson
Ulysses S. Grant
Rutherford B. Hayes

July 4, 1908 (46 stars)

Oklahoma

★

Presidents Serving under the Flag
Theodore Roosevelt
William Howard Taft

July 4, 1912 (48 stars)

New Mexico
Arizona

★

Presidents Serving under the Flag
William Howard Taft, Woodrow Wilson
Warren G. Harding, Calvin Coolidge
Herbert Hoover, Franklin D. Roosevelt
Harry S. Truman, Dwight D. Eisenhower

July 4, 1959 (49 stars)

Alaska

★

President Serving under the Flag
Dwight D. Eisenhower

July 4, 1960 (50 stars)

Hawaii

★

Presidents Serving under the Flag
Dwight D. Eisenhower, John F. Kennedy
Lyndon Johnson, Richard Nixon
Gerald Ford, Jimmy Carter
Ronald Reagan, George H. W. Bush
William Clinton, George W. Bush

SPECIAL THANKS

Thanks to Aaron Wehner and Brie Mazurek at Ten Speed Press, and to Gloria Hiek
for her dedication to designing and producing this book.

CREDITS

Copyright © 2008 by Kit Hinrichs, Delphine Hirasuna, and Terry Heffernan
Photography copyright © 2007, 2008 by Terry Heffernan
Originally published in hardcover in the United States by Ten Speed Press,
an imprint of the Crown Publishing Group, a division of Random House LLC, in 2008.

Much of the material in this book has been previously published in *Long May She Wave*
(Ten Speed Press, 2001).
Cover and text design by Kit Hinrichs/Pentagram

Library of Congress Cataloging-in-Publication Data
Hinrichs, Kit. 100 American Flags: a unique collection of Old Glory memorabilia / collection &
design by Kit Hinrichs; text by Delphine Hirasuna; photography by Terry Heffernan.
"Much of the material in this book has been previously published in *Long May She Wave*."
Summary: "A full-color photographic book presenting 100 American flag artifacts, artworks, and
memorabilia from one of the world's most eminent collectors."—Provided by publisher.
p. cm.
ISBN-13: 978-0-38536-478-2
ISBN-10: 0-38536-478-4
1. Flags in art.   2. Art, American—Pictorial works.   3. Flags—United States—Pictorial works.
4. Hinrichs, Kit—Art collections—Pictorial works.   5. Art—Private collections—United States—Pictorial works.
I. Hirasuna, Dephine, 1946–   II. Heffernan, Terry.   III. Title.   IV. Title: One hundred American flags.
N8217.F55H5595 2008
929.9'20973—dc22   2007049871

Printed in China
Proprietary Edition, 2015 Ten Speed Press
1 2 3 4 5 6 7 8 9 10